games people play!

Russia

William Lychack

CHILDREN'S PRESS®
A Division of Grolier Publishing
New York • London • Hong Kong • Sydney
Danbury, Connecticut

Design Staff

Design and Electronic Composition:
  TJS Design

Maps: TJS Design

Cover Art and Icons: Susan Kwas

Library of Congress Cataloging-in-Publication Data

Lychack, William.
Russia / by William Lychack.
  p. cm. — (Games people play)
Includes bibliographical references and index.
Summary: Surveys the sports and games played in Russia, from centuries
ago through the Soviet era but with an emphasis on on the present day.
ISBN 0-516-04441-9
1. Sports—Russia (Federation)—History—Juvenile literature. 2. Games—
Russia (Federation) [1. Sports—Russia (Federation) 2. Games—Russia
(Federation)] I. Title. II. Series.

GV623.L93 1996   96-31126
796'.0947—dc20   CIP
                                AC

Table of ontents

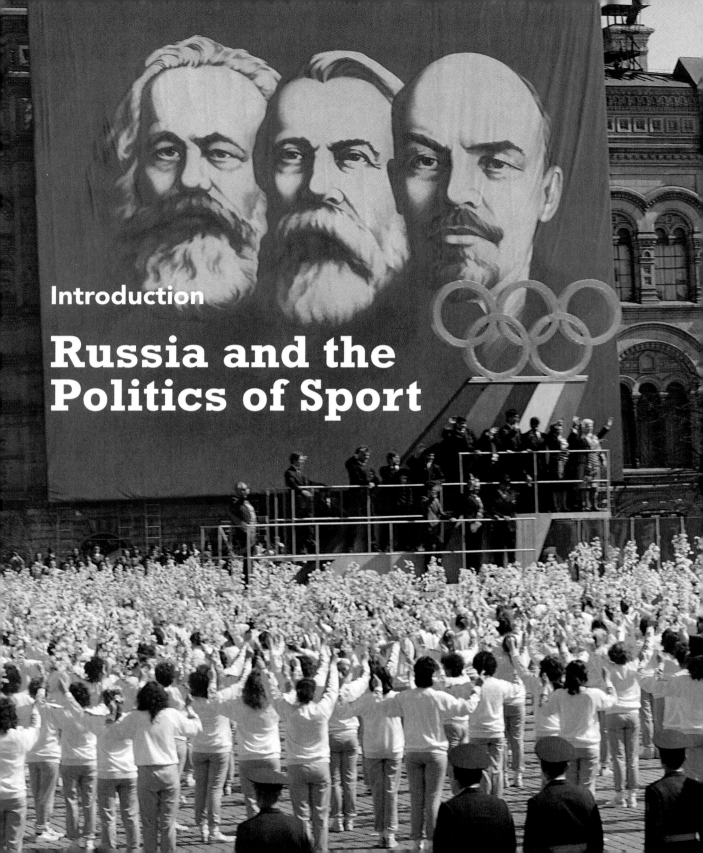

Introduction

Russia and the Politics of Sport

In the Soviet era, athletics were an important part of life. Above: Women work out in the 1950s. Opposite Page: A May Day festival in Moscow's Red Square included a celebration of Olympic athletics.

D espite tremendous upheavals in politics and the economy, sports remain *the* topic of conversation among Russian people. Almost everyone follows one sport or another. But like many other aspects of Russian life, being a dedicated sports fan in the world's largest country requires sacrifices.

Consider an avid ice hockey fan in Vladivostok in the far eastern region of Russia. He or she must stay up half the night to catch the championship match that is broadcast from Moscow — seven time zones away! All together, Russia stretches across a vast eleven time zones. (By comparison, the continental United States covers only four.)

Above: The Russian coat of arms
Below: The vast country of Russia includes bustling cities and such remote landscapes as this farm in Siberia.

Russia is enormous. A ride from Moscow (in Europe) to the Russian Pacific coast (in Asia) takes eight days on the famous Trans-Siberian Railroad. It's fully fitting that Russia's ancient coat of arms is a double-headed eagle — one looking east, the other looking west. Russia truly has a foot in both the Eastern and Western worlds.

Russia is changing at a dizzying pace. For decades, it was part of the communist Union of Soviet Socialist Republics (U.S.S.R.).

Soviet communist rule collapsed in the early 1990s, leaving Russia (also called the Russian Federation) still powerful and still huge. Today it is a country in transition and uproar. The government is now democratic, which means the people are more free than they were under communism.

Vladimir Lenin was the first leader of the U.S.S.R. (Soviet Union).

But the adjustment to a democratic society has been difficult and has caused hardships for many Russians. The country still struggles with housing shortages, low food supplies, few manufactured goods, inflation, unemployment, and an inefficient health-care system.

The breakup of the U.S.S.R. has also fractured its once-fine sports programs. During the Soviet era, sports teams and leagues were a guaranteed right of the people. The value of physical fitness was written into the Soviet constitution, and playing sports was seen as a patriotic duty. A fit people, it was said, were a strong people. The Soviet Union may be a thing of the past, but Russians' love of sports continues into Russia's new era.

Russia at a Glance

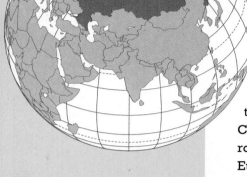

History

In centuries past, Russia has fallen to a series of conquerers, including Vikings, Romans, Poles, and Germans. Before 1917, most of Russia was controlled by rulers called tsars (also spelled czars). In 1917, Vladimir Lenin led a revolution and overthrew the tsarist government, freeing serfs and workers from bondage. The resulting government, the U.S.S.R., was based on communism, an economic and political system in which all property is owned by the people, not by individuals. In the coming decades, harsh rulers came to power and controlled all aspects of life in Russia, including the economy, education, religion, and the arts.

The Communists ruled for seventy years, and expanded their power throughout the world. Communist governments rose to power in Asia (China), Europe (Czechoslovakia), and the Western Hemisphere (Cuba). After World War II, Soviet relations with the United States were difficult, and at times the two nations came close to outright war. These were the years of the Cold War, in which the threat of nuclear war chilled diplomacy between the world's two superpowers.

In the 1980s, Soviet influence began to crumble as many communist governments in Eastern Europe were overthrown. In 1985, Mikhail Gorbachev became the new leader of the Soviet Union and began dismantling communist control of the Soviet people and economy. Gorbachev's successor, Boris Yeltsin, continued these reforms.

The Soviet Union came to an end in 1991, when the fourteen republics that were once the U.S.S.R. became independent nations called the Commonwealth of Independent States (C.I.S.). The Russian Federation (Russia) is one of those independent nations.

The Land

The Russian Federation occupies most of Eastern Europe and almost all of northern Asia. Its 6.6 million square miles (17 million square kilometers) make up about one-seventh of the earth's landmass. The Ural Mountains run through Russia, separating the continents of Europe and Asia. The famous forest known as the Taiga (woodland) is a band of ancient, thick evergreen and birch trees in the icy region of Siberia. Lake Baikal is the deepest and largest freshwater lake in the world; it is a mile deep and holds 20 percent of all the freshwater on earth.

Moscow is the spiritual, cultural, and political capital

of the Russian Federation. Its population is nearly nine million. The brightly painted city of St. Petersburg (formerly Leningrad) is one of the most beautiful cities in Europe and has a population of more than four million.

The Climate

Russia is known for its long, cold winters, but it actually sees every kind of climate on the globe (except tropics). On the cold end,

Verkhoyansk in northern Siberia is the coldest spot on earth. Its average temperature in January is 60 degrees below zero, and the ground is covered by snow for 140 to 260 days a year. At the warm end of the country, the popular resort town of Sochi sits on the Black Sea and boasts lovely, warm temperatures.

The People

There are more than 129 nationalities living in Russia.

The population is 150 million, of which 80 percent are Russians. During the Soviet era, organized religion was frowned upon. Today, the Russian Orthodox Church is thriving, as are other religious groups, including Muslims, Protestants, Roman Catholics, and Jews. The official language, Russian, is written in the Cyrillic alphabet.

Chapter One

Ice Hockey: Speed and Precision

Ice hockey is the national sport of Russia, as well as many of the former Soviet countries. Hockey is so popular in the C.I.S. that if the government wishes to make an important announcement, it usually waits until after a national broadcast of a hockey game. Otherwise, nobody would pay attention.

Ice hockey is the fastest team sport in the world. With skaters rocketing around the rink, passing the puck, and checking opponents into the boards, the action is nonstop. Teams play six to a side, including a goalie, and players use long sticks to shoot a hard rubber puck at the goal. Slap shots can reach blinding speeds of 130 miles (209 km) per hour! And incredibly enough, goalies have the nerve to keep their eyes open to stop these rifle shots. Of course, they have to wear heavy, leather padding and an unbreakable face mask.

Through the years, the Soviet Union and Russian hockey teams have dominated the Winter Olympics.

Russian children start hockey training at an early age.

puck

the small, round, black disk that hockey players pass and shoot

As in many countries today, more Russians play soccer than any other sport, but ice hockey continues to be treasured as the nation's most important sport. Russian children build their own makeshift hockey rinks in courtyards and on rivers as soon as the long winter freeze begins. After school, boys and girls gather at these rinks to practice their slap shots. They play past dusk and into the night, withstanding the frigid air. It's not unusual to hear the sounds of the puck hitting sideboards and sticks when you walk through any residential street after dark.

Russia and the Soviet Union were late in the arrival of the violent game of modern ice hockey, beginning to play the game only after World War II. But when the sport arrived, the Russians set out to build some of the greatest ice hockey teams in the world. In the Winter Olympics, the most important hockey tournament of all, the Big Red Machine of Soviet hockey never failed to win a medal. Additionally, the Russians have won more than 20 world championships since 1954.

A women's hockey team in St. Petersburg

The former-Soviet Unified Team won the 1992 Olympic gold medal in hockey (above and opposite page).

At the height of the Soviet regime, more than 800,000 young men played hockey in Russia. There were more than 40,000 teams throughout the country. Under the Russian influence, hockey was revolutionized for all the world. The high speed of play and the body contact allowed by the game made old-style hockey a game of brute force. However, the Soviets brought a precision and speed to the game that was rarely used before. With their quick, super-sharp passing and teamwork, the Soviets virtually created the game anew, relying on fitness more than muscle.

The collapse of the Soviet Union has changed Russian ice hockey forever. Many Russian teams are rapidly changing to succeed in a free market. In the communist Soviet Union, the government would pay for equipment, stadiums, and players' salaries. Now, the teams must succeed without help from the government, and they are looking for ways to make more money.

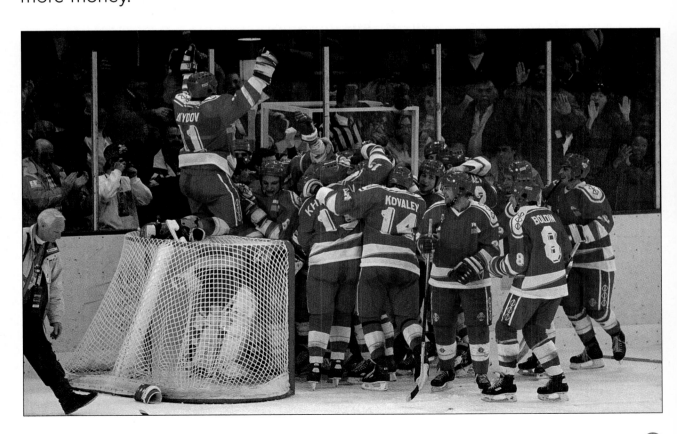

One example of the change occurring in Russian hockey is the Moscow team known as CSKA. Since 1947 they had won 33 national championships and were considered the most successful hockey team in the history of the Soviet Union. But after the collapse of the Soviet Union, money became tight, the team began losing its best players, attendance plunged, and this once-proud team finished the 1993 season last in their league. At one point, the team's coach traveled to the United States to find an American company to sponsor the team. Howard Baldwin, chairman of the Pittsburgh Penguins, formed a partnership between the CSKA and the Penguins. Now the CSKA plays with new uniforms and with a new team name: the Russian Penguins! The new Penguins play before sellout crowds in a refurbished stadium, complete with rock music and laser-light shows. Although some hard-core Russian hockey fans dislike the changes, everyone recognizes that CSKA learned a valuable lesson. Every sports team in Russia must be prepared to adapt to the new economic system.

Even those Russian teams that succeed financially find challenges they cannot meet — the drain of talent to North America. Today there are about 50 Russian players in the National Hockey League (NHL), which operates in

National Hockey League

North American professional
hockey league, known
as the NHL

Canada and the United States. In 1989, Sergei Priakin became the first athlete from the U.S.S.R. to be granted permission to play in a North American pro league. He made his debut with the NHL's Calgary Flames and opened the door for some of the finest hockey stars in the world. The highly talented 20-year-old winger Alexander Mogilny joined the Buffalo Sabres in 1989. And Sergei Makarov, one of the game's most dynamic talents, joined Priakin on the Flames. Vladimir Krutov, a left wing, and Igor Larionov, a center, play together for the Vancouver Canucks.

Pavel Bure is one of many Russian hockey players to make an impact in the NHL.

Today, during the NHL's Stanley Cup playoffs, there are likely to be as many Russian televisions tuned to the games as there are in the United States or Canada. Some NHL teams now send money to sponsor the Russian teams. This influx of talent into the NHL raised the quality of the league's play. But the drain on talent in Russia, along with the continuing Russian economic problems, has created widespread concern about the survival of high-level hockey in Russia.

Some people believe that the influx of Russian hockey players into the NHL has brought the world a little closer and made it a little more peaceful. For decades, the United States and the Soviet Union were enemies, and their sports teams met in bitter rivalries at the Olympics. Now, Russians are playing in the United States, and the American national pastime, baseball, is catching on in Russia. Peter Stastny, a Czechoslovakian playing on the Quebec Nordiques said, "I really believe this and other things that we hear are happening [in Russia] tell us that we are heading into a nice, peaceful period in the history of mankind."

Opposite page: A Russian girl straps on her shoulder pads in preparation for a hockey game.

Bears and Hockey and the Circus?

Since ice hockey is the national sport of Russia and the brown bear is the national animal, it's not surprising to see bears playing hockey.

Or is it?

You be the judge! At center ice, "Bruins Play Hockey," a circus attraction with the beloved Moscow ice troupe!

The famous Russian Circus originated in the steady flow of clowns and acrobats who entertained the court of Empress Anna in the early eighteenth century. The bear, in Russia, is thought of as sacred. In the past, people were not allowed to say the bear's name out loud, for fear they might raise the bear's anger against the village. Today, the original word for bear is lost in Russian. They call him medved (pronounced mid-VID), meaning "the one who knows where the honey is." But you can still read about Bruin the bear in the famous fable "Reynard the Fox." So we do know where teams such as the Boston Bruins of the NHL get their name.

Chapter Two

More Team Sports:
Soccer, Basketball,
Volleyball

A soccer player for the
Kiev Dynamos

Soccer is, in fan appeal, the most popular sport across most of the former Soviet Union. People follow their teams fanatically. Graffiti of team logos and players' names is scrawled in Cyrillic letters along staircases and on factory walls. The leading soccer teams, such as Moscow Spartak and Kiev Dynamo, continually perform well in world and European tournaments. And football matches draw capacity crowds.

Soccer was first introduced in Russia when foreign residents, mostly British and Germans, played among themselves and on mixed teams. Western college students and others living in Russia formed the Victoria Football Club in St. Petersburg during the 1880s, but they did not play against any Russians. It wasn't until 1892 that the first soccer match among Russians was recorded. The sport became so popular that by 1912, the Russian Football Association sent a

Soviet fans cheer on the national soccer team during a 1980s match.

team to the Olympic Games in Sweden. Unfortunately their debut was a disaster — they were defeated by Germany 16–0!

Since the Soviets seized power in 1917, soccer was promoted as an excellent example of teamwork, an ideal cherished by the communist government. Soviet leaders believed that if the people had good role models in soccer team players, then society itself would benefit. Soccer leagues and tournaments were heavily supported and sponsored by the government.

Russian soccer matches are usually more subdued than many of those in Western Europe. One reason is that the sale of alcohol is forbidden at Russian games. This helps prevent the "hooliganism" and violence that has marred the European game since it was developed centuries ago. Some 2,000 years ago, Roman conquerors brought an ancient ball game called "harpastum" with them everywhere they went, and one of those places was the Black Sea area of Russia. As the game developed in Europe, it turned so violent in England that it was outlawed for a time.

Soviet coach Anatoli Bychovets is tossed in the air by his team after the Russians won the Olympic gold medal in soccer.

World Cup

international soccer tournament held every four years

The absence of alcohol at Russian games helps keep the crowds under control. But for years under the Soviet regime, a steel line of soldiers ringed the soccer field, facing the crowd throughout the game. These imposing faces served as a warning against rowdy behavior, and the politeness of Russian soccer crowds continues today. However, when Tbilisi won the Soviet National Cup one year, thousands of people poured into the streets of the Georgian capital, dancing and cheering. Russian soldiers were called in to quiet the celebration.

The Soviets never won the famed World Cup, but they have fared better in the Olympics. Their 1988 team won the gold medal over Brazil on the fast-break attack in overtime by substitute Yuri Savichev of Moscow. Many of Russia's finest players have emigrated to play professionally in the West.

Like many other western games, **tennis** is gaining popularity in Russia. People love to play tennis, but it is hard to find a court on which to play. Boris Yeltsin, currently president of the Russian Federation, is a passionate tennis buff.

In 1959, Nikita Khrushchev prepared the Soviet Union for its first state visit from an American president, Dwight D. Eisenhower. Khrushchev had a **golf** course built for Eisenhower, the first (and also the last) ever built in the country. Due to political reasons, however, the trip was cancelled by the United States.

Russian president Boris Yeltsin works out on the tennis court.

Russia's Yevgeny Kafelnikov entered the top rank of world tennis players when he won the 1996 French Open tournament.

Baseball (above), the national pastime in the United States, is gaining a following in Russia. The country's first national baseball championships were held in 1989. And volleyball (right) is quite popular, too. The Soviet Union won 12 medals in Olympic volleyball competition.

The favorite American sport to take hold in Russia is **basketball**. Modern basketball was devised in 1891 by Dr. James Naismith in Springfield, Massachusetts. The sport developed slowly over the next several decades. But since the 1940s, it has grown in popularity, and it is now the most popular professional sport in the United States. Basketball is spreading around the world, too. Russia and Eastern Europe are not immune to its excitement and world-famous stars.

Because it is a fast-paced, no-contact game, basketball has long been a popular conditioning sport in Russia. The game was played as a warm-up exercise by women gymnasts and male wrestlers in the famous Soviet sports schools.

Russian and American women duel in Olympic basketball.

Again, like many other modern sports, basketball became quite popular in the Soviet Union in part because of the exposure it received in the Olympics. The game was added to Summer Olympic play in 1936, and the Soviets rose to contend for the gold medal every four years.

One of the most dramatic and controversial moments in Olympic history was the 1972 basketball gold-medal game between the Soviet Union and the United States. The Soviets beat the Americans 51–50 for the gold, breaking a 63-game U.S. winning streak. The Americans complained because they believed the Russians' winning basket should have been negated because of a timekeeper's error. The Soviets again won basketball gold in 1988, and almost all of that team's star players went on to sign contracts with the National Basketball Association in the United States. Others signed with clubs in Spain and Germany.

Basketball came to Russia in the first half of the 20th century. Once the Soviet government was established in the 1910s, the Soviet Red Army launched a military campaign to the east in which it conquered several other European countries, including Latvia, Lithuania, and Estonia. While occupying these countries, the Russians observed that the YMCA had set up gymnasiums where locals flocked indoors to

Red Army

the national army
of the Soviet Union

In the 1972 Olympic gold-medal game, the U.S. team thought it had won (left), but a timekeeper's error reversed the final score and gave the win to the Soviets (above).

play Western games such as basketball and volleyball. Vigorous, entertaining indoor sports made a lot of sense to the Russians, who could not play outdoor sports for much of the year. Beginning in the 1940s, basketball and volleyball had spread across the Soviet Union and are still played enthusiastically today.

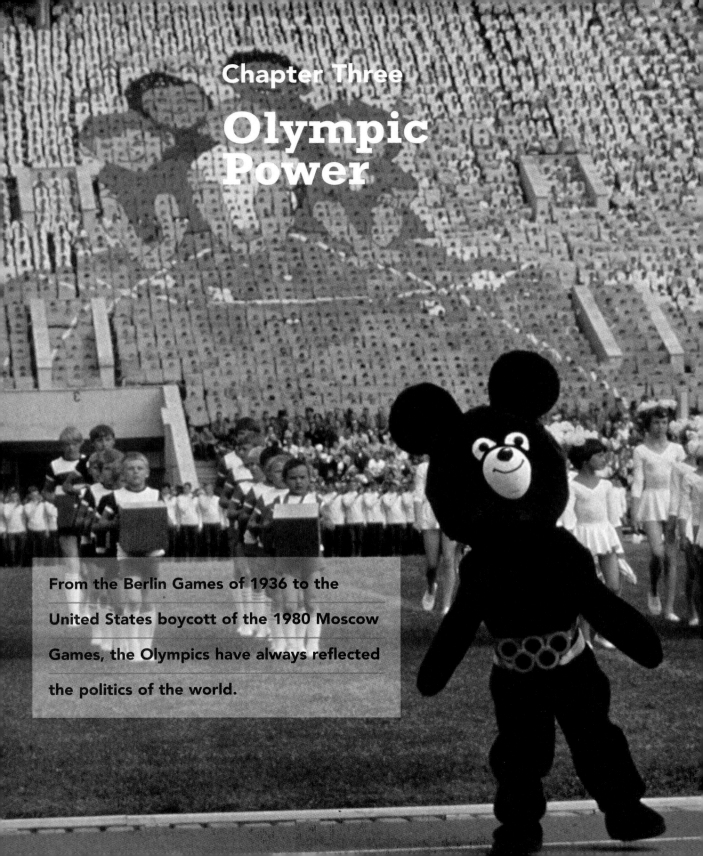

Chapter Three
Olympic Power

From the Berlin Games of 1936 to the United States boycott of the 1980 Moscow Games, the Olympics have always reflected the politics of the world.

I n all the world, there are just two places where people from all countries gather together — the United Nations and the Olympics. The United Nations is a political organization devoted to international peace and cooperation. Much the same has been said of the Olympics, which are held every four years.

During the Cold War, the Olympics became the prime arenas for the rivalry between the Soviet-controlled countries and the Western democracies, such as the United States. An Olympic medal meant not just an athletic victory, but a political triumph as well. With great personal and political pride, contestants from the Soviet Union were clearly the best-trained athletes that ever played modern sports.

Having joined the Olympics in 1952, the Soviet Union harvested nearly 1,700 medals — nearly five hundred of which were gold. After the breakup of the Soviet Union, the countries of the former U.S.S.R. participated under the name of the Unified Team in the 1992 Olympics. Beginning with the time of the 1994 Winter Olympics, the former Soviet countries were competing as independent nations.

Tatyana Goutsou, who competed for the Unified Team in the 1992 Olympics.

Opposite Page: Opening ceremonies for the 1980 Summer Olympic Games, which were held in Moscow.

The Summer Olympic Games, as held today, would be quite familiar and recognizable to the ancient Greeks who started them more than four thousand years ago. Several factors make the Olympics very modern — women compete in addition to men; some events are scored with sophisticated electronic timing sensors; and the games are seen on television by billions of people around the world. But many of the events, especially in track and field, are direct descendants of the ancient games.

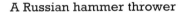

A Russian hammer thrower

In 1894, when Tsarist Russia gathered with eleven other countries to revive the Olympics, **track and field** athletics became the central core of the modern games. Because speed, strength, agility, and endurance are so openly tested by the varied events — some of which include walk, sprint, hurdle, relay races, marathons,

Vladimir Kuts runs in the 1956
Olympics

long jumps, high jumps, triple jumps, as well as
javelin, hammer, and discus throws — track
and field events are perhaps the most popular
sports at the Olympics. *Citius, altius, fortius*
("faster, higher, stronger"), the ancient Greek
motto, perfectly sums up what track and field
tasks bring out in athletes.

In the "faster" category, the dramatic long-
distance runner Vladimir Kuts remains one of
the Soviet Union's most celebrated medalists.

In the 1956 Olympics, Kuts faced England's Gordon Pirie in a 10,000-meter race that was billed as the race of the Melbourne, Australia, Games. Four months before their Olympic meeting, Kuts lost to Pirie in the final stretch. But two months later, Kuts set the world record. This Olympic race was to be their duel, and radios were tuned to the race around the world.

From the starting gun, Kuts took the lead. But halfway through the race, the Soviet runner went through a series of dramatic sprints and jogs. His strategy was to break Pirie's concentration. By the end, Pirie was so beaten by the tactics that he finished eighth!

"He murdered me," Pirie later said. "I couldn't take that switching pace. It was torture."

What Kuts demonstrated to the world was the Russian ability to withstand torture. The Russian sportswriter Yuri Brokhin observed, "Kuts was a Russian peasant — a unique branch of mankind that has survived silently through four centuries of Mongol hordes, three centuries of tsars, and sixty years of Soviet Communism."

Soviet Vyacheslav Ivanenko etched his name in the long list of Soviet medal winners in 1988. But he didn't run, lift, or throw anything — he just walked, a skill he learned well in his home of Siberia. The Russian walked 3 miles (5 km) to and from his job because it was good exercise for his bad back. The exercise paid off. In the Olympics, he won a gold medal in the 50-meter walk. In walking events, racers are required to keep their feet in constant contact with the ground, so before the toe of one foot leaves the ground, the heel of the other foot must touch down.

In the "higher" category, Russia has long dominated the field events of the pole vault and triple jump. In the vault in 1988, for instance, the Unified Team swept all the medals, as champion Sergei Bubka won the gold. In the triple jump, contestants take off and land on the same foot, take a step onto the other foot, and then jump. The event used to be called the "hop, skip, and jump," which is an accurate description. The Soviet team's extraordinary jumper Viktor Saneyev won the gold medals in 1968, 1972, and 1976. In 1980, Saneyev lost his bid for four straight gold medals when he lost to Jaak Uudmae, his Soviet teammate.

In the 1964 Summer Olympics, Valery Brumel (left) narrowly defeated American John Thomas for the gold medal in the high jump. Despite the Cold War, the two competitors became friends.

A year after his Olympic triumph, Brumel was in a terrible motorcycle accident. His right leg was broken in many places and his foot was left barely attached. In the hospital, a devastated Brumel received the following telegram from John Thomas: *Sometimes a twist of fate seems to have been put there to test a man's strength of character. Don't admit defeat. I sincerely hope you come back to jump again.*

Brumel kept the letter at his side during the many operations and months of conditioning ahead. Eventually, he did jump again. Brumel never reached the championship level again, but the strength and friendship he earned through sports allowed him to achieve in the face of hardship.

Legendary Russian
weightlifter Vasili Alexeyev

In their ancient fables, Russian heroes are celebrated for their physical strength. And, like the folk tales of old, the Russians have dominated almost all areas of Olympic strength. In the "stronger" category, the hammer throw is an interesting event that Russians dominate in virtually every Olympics. They have won the gold medal in all but two Olympics since 1954. The fact is that the Soviet Union missed one of those years only because they boycotted the Los Angeles Games in 1984, after the United States had boycotted the Soviet games in 1980.

Weightlifting competitions with stone weights were present at the first Olympics in Greece. In carnivals, crowds watched as the professional strongman lifted horse wagons and armloads of people. The modern weightlifter uses two types of lifts, the "snatch" and the "jerk." One of the strongest lifters of all time was super-heavyweight Russian Vasili Alexeyev, who won eight world championships.

Gymnastics, like track and field, find their source in the educational system of the Greeks of Athens. The word comes from the ancient Greek word *gymnsion*, which means "a place to exercise naked." Today's gymnasts wear clothes when they twist and twirl through the air, but athletes are still rigorously judged by the time-less standards of grace, strength, and precision.

Because they are so commit-ted to their training, young Russian gymnasts are always among the medal winners at the Olympics.

Men and women compete separately, with six types of exercises for men and four for women. The men's events include the parallel bars, horizontal bar, floor exercise, pommel horse, rings, and vault. The women's exercises are the vault, uneven bars, balance beam, and floor exercise. Under the spotlight of televison, gymnastics has grown in popularity in both Russia and the world.

Under the Soviet system, children with special athletic talents were enrolled in special sports schools at very early ages. There were more than 5,500 such schools, specializing in a particular sport or group of sports. Under this school system, the Soviet Union produced generation after generation of champions, including gymnasts. Many of these schools still exist, although their future is uncertain in the democratic Russia.

Vitaly Scherbo

Between 1956 and 1964, the female gymnast Larissa Latynina won a record 18 Olympic medals, 9 of which were gold. The record for most gymnastics medals for a male, 15, is held by Nikolai Andriano; 7 of his were gold. In recent years, the Russian king of gymnastics is Vitaly Scherbo, who won an incredible six gold medals (all-around, parallel bars, vault, pommel horse, rings, and as part of the winning Unified Team) at the 1988 Olympics.

But no Russian athlete will ever erase the memory of the all-time darling of Soviet gymnastics, Olga Korbut. In the 1950s and 1960s, the Soviets, though perfect in their execution of programs, were often judged as too cold and machine-like in their performances. Olga Korbut changed all of that. She introduced her lively personality into the flawless Soviet team and won the gold in the 1972 floor exercises, balance beam, and a silver in the uneven bars. She led her team to the overall gold medal that year.

Olga Korbut

The Winter Olympic Games began in 1924, when they were introduced at the Olympics in Chamonix, France. With Russia's excessively cold climate, the Winter Games suit its athletes well. And, more than any other worldwide event, the Winter Olympics have left their permanent mark upon Russia. In fact, many of Russia's most popular winter sports come directly from the country's fierce preparation for the Winter Games. Many historians maintain that Russia's national sport, hockey, might never have taken hold in the country had it not been an Olympic sport.

Long Russian winters lead many young people to find fun and games in the most difficult weather conditions.

A Russian biathlete prepares to shoot.

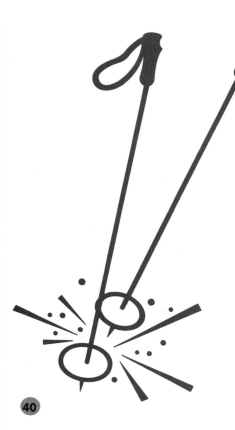

Biathlon competitions combine two sports— cross country skiing and rifle marksmanship —into one grueling event. The modern sport grew first from hunting and later from military training for soldiers in Scandinavia. What makes the biathlon so challenging is its combination of strenuous skiing, and then stopping to hold a gun steady to shoot at small targets. Alone, cross-country skiing events require great upper-body strength and fitness to double-pole across level terrain. But for the biathlete, the task is twice as hard, because he or she must race between the shooting ranges and then lower his or her heart rate in order to accurately sight the rifle. Competitors who miss targets must ski penalty laps of 150 meters.

It's not surprising that the Russians have taken the sport into their hearts. In the tradition of "physical culture" in the Soviet Union, no high school student could have graduated without proving that he or she could cover several kilometers of snow-covered terrain on skis in a certain time limit. Combine that with the fine hunting known in the Russian forests and the government's strong military, and there's no question that the Russians would be naturally inclined to the biathlon.

Snowy conditions in Siberia help prepare Russians for international skiing competitions.

The fact, however, is not that the people are merely inclined to the sport. The Russians have made the sport hugely popular during the long, snow-covered winters. A biathlon in Minsk, Belarus, will regularly draw more than 50,000 people. In the United States, by contrast, biathletes rarely see more than a hundred spectators. Again, like most Olympic competitions, the Russians dominate the biathlon. Since the sport was introduced in 1960, the Soviet team has missed only one gold medal in the relay.

Ice skating is a popular activity in Russia — for fun and in competition. One of the most famous Russian figure-skating pairs was Ludmila Belousova and Oleg Proptopopov (below), who competed for the Soviet Union in the 1960s.

Figure skating has long been popular in the former Soviet Union. The first world championships were held in St. Petersburg in 1896. During Russia's long tradition in the sport, their skaters have revolutionized and led the world. The Soviet skaters Ludmila Belousova and Oleg Proptopopov introduced classical ballet to pairs dancing. Recently, Viktor Petrenko of the Unified Team (1992) and Alexai Urmanov of the Russian team (1994) won the gold in the men's individual competition. The beautiful and artistic Oksana Baiul of the Unified Team won the women's gold medal in 1994. Baiul, of the Ukraine (a member of the C.I.S.), summed up why she likes the sport of figure skating: "One should not be afraid to lose, this is a sport. One day you win, another day you lose. Of course, everyone wants to be the best. This is normal. This is what sport is about. This is why I love it."

Oksana Baiul, who skated for the Unified Team in the early 1990s

Chapter Four

Chess and Other Challenges of the Mind

I n its distinguished history of more than nine centuries, Russia has produced some of the most outstanding artists and scientists in the world. From the great literature of Leo Tolstoy to the paintings of Marc Chagall, the culture of Russia is deep and wide. Contributing to this intellectual rigor is Russia's close attention to the demanding game of **chess** and such other strategy games as backgammon and dominoes.

Chess, the queen of all board games, is a thinking person's game of war. Each chess piece represents units in an army, and a player's object is to capture the other player's king. This is called "checkmate." Chess is easy to learn, difficult to master, and has cast a strong spell over nearly everyone who has ever played the game seriously. As proof, chess has been the subject of more books than all other games combined. On average, there is a chess book published every single day somewhere in the world.

Needless to say, chess has been considered the national game of many countries since its invention in India more than 1,300 years ago. The game arrived in Russia by way of trade with

Opposite Page: In some Russian schools, chess is part of the regular curriculum.

A favorite Russian pastime is chess in a public park.

the Vikings, who had learned the game from the Persians. The name "chess" is derived from the Persian word *shah* ("king" or "ruler").

As is true of most old games like chess, there are age-old laws of playing that one must observe. For instance, if you touch one of your pieces, you must play it — you cannot move another. And a move is considered over when you take you fingers off the piece you move.

It would be an understatement to say that chess is popular among Russians. Chess is an obsession! Everywhere you look, people are playing chess. Everyone plays the game in trains, restaurants, hotel lobbies, at picnics. Nearly every public park has a well-kept, quiet corner devoted to chess players. There are large-scale chess matches in parks in which the pieces are sometimes taller than people! Never dull, there are many hundreds of chess clubs and chess newspapers and journals. Millions of players take part in the national tournaments. The Russian players have had a lock on the world chess rankings for decades.

In the former Soviet Union, champion chess players are celebrities. Chess players are stars, much like a basketball player in the U.S. or a soccer player in Brazil. The best Russian chess player can earn large amounts in prize money. At the highest level, chess is a full-time job.

A Russian chess tournament

New York City

INTERSCO

A. KARPOV

One of the most famous series of chess matches this century was in the 1970s between the American Bobby Fischer and the Russian Boris Spassky (right). This tournament was viewed as a Cold War test between the two superpowers. In the 1980s and 1990s, Russian masters Anatoli Karpov and Gari Kasparov faced off in a series of championship matches (above).

BORIS
SPASSKY

BOBBY
FISC

THE WORLD CHESS CHAMPIONSHIP

In 1988, Russian chess master Gari Kasparov played several simultaneous chess games against schoolchildren in New York City.

The physical and mental demands of top tournament play are such that the players must be supremely fit — physically and mentally.

In the 1986 World Championship series between the two famous Russian masters, Anatoli Karpov and Gari Kasparov, the world was treated to a glimpse of life as a chess grand master. The challenger, Karpov, was supported by three world-class players, a personal doctor, a translator, secretary, and physical trainer. The champion, Kasparov, soldiered on with only two assistants (called "seconds"), his mother, and a couple of friends. Karpov, a brilliant man with prominent cheekbones and a high-pitched voice, lost the match. So much for his entourage.

grand master

a top-ranked chess champion

Backgammon is a lusty, fun-filled game in Russia. Dice are thrown down hard against the side of the board, and pieces are slammed and flung about. The Russians play backgammon quickly, barely exchanging a grunt with one another as they grumble and gamble over the game.

A 1990 international backgammon tournament held in Russia.

Nobody is certain of backgammon's origins. The legends surrounding the game tend to confuse its real history. The best evidence credits the Romans. They were avid players of a game called *duodecim scripta,* which was later modified to *tabula.* This game spread across Europe under the name of "tables" and led to modern backgammon.

Whatever the truth, backgammon blends strategic play with the excitement of a race game. One of the most fascinating things about backgammon is its board. Being a race game, it's not surprising that the backgammon board has 24 "points," like the 24 hours of the day. There are 12 points on each half of the board, like the 12 months of the year. And there are 30 playing pieces, like the days in a month. Day and night might be the two dice that are thrown.

Dominoes is more a ritual than just a game in Russia. It is a deeply meditative game, but it can be highly spirited as well. Often, the Russians will place friendly wagers on their dominoes games. And sometimes, the game is played in the tea houses and restaurants so that a loser can be found to buy the next round of *kvass*, a popular beer-like drink.

As the game pieces illustrate, dominoes is a game derived from dice. The pieces are usually called "bones," and there are 28 of them in a set (or "deck"). This deck includes tiles for the 21 pairings of two dice, plus seven tiles matching a blank with a die and with another blank. To play, the bones are put facedown on a table and shuffled. Two players draw seven tiles each (up to four players can play). The remaining tiles remain facedown in the boneyard. After the first player sets his or her piece, the second player matches one end of a bone in his or her hand with one end of the set on the table.

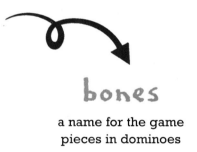

bones

a name for the game
pieces in dominoes

The Russians play a variation of standard dominoes called, appropriately, Russian dominoes. It is also known as "all sevens" and "matador." In this version, a player can draw from the boneyard even when he or she holds a playable piece in hand. This tiny change in the rules shifts the game from one of luck to one of supreme strategy.

Chapter Five

Zakal and the Pastimes of the People

The Russian bather does not go to a public bath just to get clean. A trip to the banya is a true event. The entire process is what Russians cherish.

Many Russians take baths in communal facilities. These public baths are a perfect illustration of the genius that is the Russian mind. The **banya** ("bath house") takes the Northern European sauna and combines it with the steamy, Eastern-oriented baths known throughout Turkey. But the Russian baths add their own healthy dose of Russian suffering!

The process begins in making the excursion to the bath. When the bather arrives, she or he is greeted by the exotic beauty of the bath house itself. Built before the revolution of 1917, many banyi (plural of banya) are filled with baroque and gilded moldings, big marble staircases, and huge, ceiling-to-floor mirrors.

The bather undresses and begins the careful ritual of the bath. The bather is weighed, soaps up, steams, rinses, and then sits in the sauna to sweat. It is believed that sweating in the sauna removes "impurities" from the body. In this hot room, fire-heated bricks reach oven-like temperatures. Water is poured on the bricks to create steam.

sauna

steam bath in which the steam comes from water poured on hot bricks

Opposite page: Visitors at a traditional Russian bath

Polar bear club swimmers often involve the entire family.

Bathers receive massages from attendants in the baths. They can take mud baths and salt baths, and they can purchase little bundles of birch branches. With these, they hit their skin with the fragrant leaves, and then rinse off with ice-cold water. The process, they say, cures most diseases.

A chilly variation on the Russian banya are the many walrus and polar bear clubs that hold meetings throughout Russia. The members of a polar bear club skip the bath house and go straight to a near-freezing river. Swimming is very popular in Russia — the country has more than 2,500 public pools. But that is perhaps not enough. Members of the Polar Bear Club of Moscow live for *zakal*, a word meaning "winter fitness" in Russian. The members will, in the middle of winter, jog down to the banks of the icy Muskva River in Moscow, cut a hole in the ice, rub themselves down with snow, and take a dip. They say it is thoroughly invigorating.

All the while, in both the baths and at the frozen riverside, there is the constant banter of small talk and joking between the bathers. As always, there is a game of chess being played. Or there are the card games that many Russians love — bridge, cribbage, and especially whist. At the beginning of the 20th century, whist was known as the most popular Russian card game. Like chess, Russian whist is a game of intense strategy. Known to Russians as *vint*, whist is a complicated game of cards in which four players, two against two, play for trumps and race to be the first team to reach 500 points. It is, above all, a game of the mind; thus, it is widely enjoyed in Russia.

Russian children jumping rope

Childhood in Russia is similar to childhood most anywhere in the world: days filled with games, toy guns, dolls, school homework, and household chores. In Russia, childhood is a cherished time. If anything, parents tend to be overprotective of their children. This custom, as can be seen in the swaddling of small children, comes out of old Russia.

In those days, the climate made a child's survival a constant question. Even today, many children and adults die from illnesses that are curable in the West. This is due to the harsh nature of life in the former Soviet Union. One result of this constant watching-over and tending-to is that children in Russia are very well behaved, but sometimes also spoiled. They are read to very often, as reading and education are highly appreciated values in Russia.

Acrobats in the
Moscow Circus

For fun, one of a Russian child's favorite treats is to attend the world-famous Moscow Circus, with its acrobats and tigers and bears and clowns. There are a great many puppet theaters throughout the countryside. Here, puppeteers retell cherished Russian fables and sing songs to accordion music.

A favorite Russian children's activity is making dolls out of corn husks.

At home, children play with dolls in both summer and winter, as they do in most other countries of the world. In rural Russia, peasant parents will often carve wooden dolls for their children. The most famous of these dolls are the *matryoshka*, the famous nesting dolls of Russia. But other dolls are made of straw, clay, and fabric. These look quite lifelike with traditional dress and the kerchief that most Russian women in the country wear. Many young boys will keep their "moss men" all their life. These are dolls made from moss and string.

Some other common games among children in Russia are Russian scandal, in which players form a line or a circle and one player whispers a "rumor" into the ear of the next. The game is recognizable to American children as very similar to the game of telephone. Similarly, Russian children love to play leapfrog, hopscotch, pat-a-cake, and jacks. These games are loved universally by children on almost every continent.

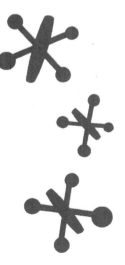

A skateboarder in Leningrad

In the cities, it is not unusual to find the same sorts of games that kids play in the United States such as handball, skateboarding, and video games. One of the most popular video games in the world, Tetris, was created in Russia by a computer programmer named Alexey Pajitnov. The challenge of Tetris, it is often said, is to stop playing!

Eskimos

groups of people who live in cold weather regions of eastern Siberia, Greenland, northern Canada, and Alaska

In the far reaches of Siberia, Russian Eskimo children play a target game called *nuglutang*. This game comes from the long winters of the Arctic, where darkness reigns for many months of the year. The Eskimos use a long, thin piece of caribou antler as the target. They then drill a dozen holes in the target and tie it to a string and hang it from a ceiling. All the players stand under the hanging target and try to put their antler into one of the holes. The object is to be the first player to get your antler through one of the holes.

Because Russian winters are so long and so fierce, spring is celebrated with joyous festivals and holidays. Among the most important is Easter. At Easter, Russians and Ukrainians busy themselves making elaborate and beautiful *psysanka* eggs. Though the children help to make these Easter eggs, they have more fun playing their own sport of egg jousting with their precious allotment of eggs.

In egg jousting, it is not a question of if your eggs will break. Rather, it is a dilemma of *when* they will break. The eggs are dyed in the traditional color of red. An egg, of course, has an anatomy, which is used in this game. There is the head of the egg, the pointed end; and there is the heel, the rounded end. The players take their egg and challenge their opponent by saying, "With my heel I will break your heel." Or: "With my head I will break your head." If the player accepts the challenge, he or she says, "Then break it," and holds out the egg to be hit. If the egg cracks, the opponent must turn over the egg, and it is hit yet again. If the challenged egg does not break, the turn ends and the eggs are exchanged. When both ends of the player's egg have been broken, the winning player captures the broken egg.

Russian *psysanka* eggs made for Easter

When they reach school, Russian children are encouraged to play organized sports, such as soccer or gymnastics. Many of Russia's best athletes start very young, and it is not unusual for an eight-year-old girl to be an aspiring ballerina, dreaming of performing in "Swan Lake" for the Bolshoi Ballet.

Glossary

acrobats
gymnasts or circus performers who do amazing feats with their bodies

backgammon
two-player board game using dice and round game pieces

banya
Russian bath house where people enjoy a mixture of steam and the dry heat of a sauna

biathlon
competition that combines cross-country skiing and rifle shooting

boycott
to refuse to trade or visit a country or event

Cold War
conflict between the Soviet Union and the United States from the 1950s to the 1980s that was fought through politics and threats, not with weapons

communism
economic and political system in which all property is owned by the people, not by individuals, and leaders are chosen by a ruling party

cribbage
popular counting card game

Cyrillic alphabet
letters in which Russian and other Eastern European languages are written

egg jousting
Easter game in which each player wins an opponent's egg by cracking it

football
term for "soccer" used in most of the world (as opposed to American football)

grand master
expert chess player

harpastum
ancient ball game brought to Russia and other countries by the Romans; the basis of soccer

hooligan
rough, violent person who causes trouble and does not care about the safety of others

kvass
a drink similar to beer

matryoshka
"nesting" dolls; hollowed-out, wooden dolls that are carved to fit within one another

medved
modern word for "bear"; its actual meaning is "the one who knows where the honey is"

moss men
straw-like dolls

nugutang
Siberian target game that uses caribou antlers

psysanka
decorated Easter eggs

Russian Orthodox Church
the most common religion in Russia

snatch
a weightlifting term meaning "to lift"

superpowers
term that refers to the Soviet Union and the United States during the Cold War

tsars (or czars)
kings who ruled Russia until the Revolution of 1917

vint
Russian word for whist, a popular card game

zakal
term for "winter fitness" referring to swimmers who enjoy ice-cold water

Books

Andrews, William G. **The Land and People of the Soviet Union**. HarperCollins, 1991.

Bellow, Bob. **Gymnastics**. Franklin Watts, 1992.

Coffey, Wayne. **Olga Korbut**. Blackbirch, 1992.

Duden, Jane. **Men's and Women's Gymnastics**. Macmillan, 1992.

Gutman, Bill. **Ice Hockey**. Marshall Cavendish, 1990.

Harris, Jack. **The Winter Olympics**. Creative Education, 1990.

Harvey, Miles. **The Fall of the Soviet Union**. Children's Press, 1995.

Howard, Dale. **Soccer Around the World**. Children's Press, 1994.

Sandelson, Robert. **Ice Sports**. Macmillan, 1991.

Wergin, Joseph P. **Cribbage for Kids**. International Gamester, 1990.

Online Sites

CSKA of Moscow
http://www.quark.lu.se/~oxana/teams/csk.html
Home page for the Russian soccer team CSKA, which has been in existence since 1923.

National News Service
http://www.nnsru/engind.html
English version of Russia's news agency website

Omni Glass
http://www.usnetcraft.com/omniglass/
Features hand-painted Easter eggs, matryoshka dolls, action toys, and other Russian crafts.

Russian National Football League
http://www.quark.lu.se/~oxana/main.html
Information, scores, standings, and player profiles for the top soccer league in Russia.

Torpedo
http://www.garoslavl.su/~maksim/hockey.html
Home page of the Russian hockey team Torpedo

Virtual Gallery of St. Petersburg Artists
http://www.visor.com/info/art.html
Website devoted to exposing Russian artists to the world.

Index

About the Author
William Lychack works in Minneapolis, Minnesota, as a writer and editor. He was educated at Connecticut College and the University of Michigan. He has taught at the University of Michigan, Middlebury College, and the University of Minnesota, and he has been an editor at *New England Review*. His fiction has appeared in many quarterly magazines, including *Ascent, Seattle Review, Witness, Quarterly West,* and others. He has lived, for short periods of time, in London.